D1058295

by W·H·AUDEN

CITY WITHOUT WALLS

WALLS

and Other Poems

W·H·AUDEN

CITY WITHOUT WALLS
and Other Poems

RANDOM HOUSE NEW YORK

Some of these poems first appeared in
The Atlantic Monthly, Confrontation, Delos,
Encounter, The New York Review of Books, The Quest,
The London Magazine, and *The London Observer.*
"The Twelve" was written for a musical setting
by Sir William Walton and is reprinted by permission
of the publisher, Oxford University Press.
Copyright © 1966 by Oxford University Press.
The following poems appeared originally in
The New Yorker: "Epithalamium," "The Horatians,"
"Fairground," and "City Without Walls."

First Printing
2, 3, 4, 5, 6, 7, 8, 9

Library of Congress Catalog Card Number: 71–85584

Manufactured in the United States of America
by The Book Press, Brattleboro, Vermont
Designed by Andrew Roberts
Binding design by Anita Karl

for PETER HEYWORTH

At Twenty we find our friends for ourselves, but it takes Heaven
To find us one when we are Fifty-Seven

CONTENTS

vii

CITY WITHOUT
WALLS
and Other Poems

City Without Walls

... "Those fantastic forms, fang-sharp,
     bone-bare, that in Byzantine painting
     were a shorthand for the Unbounded
     beyond the Pale, unpolicied spaces
     where dragons dwelt and demons roamed,

"colonized only by ex-worldlings,
     penitent sophists and sodomites,
     are visual facts in the foreground now,
     real structures of steel and glass:
     hermits, perforce, are all today,

"with numbered caves in enormous jails,
     hotels designed to deteriorate
     their glum already-corrupted guests,
     factories in which the functional
     Hobbesian Man is mass-produced.

"A key to the street each convict has,
     but the Asphalt Lands are lawless marches

where gangs clash and cops turn
robber-barons: reckless he
who walks after dark in that wilderness.

"But electric lamps allow nightly
cell meetings where subcultures
may hold palaver, like-minded,
their tongues tattooed by the tribal jargon
of the vice or business that brothers them;

"and mean cafés to remain open,
where in bad air belly-talkers,
weedy-looking, work-shy,
may spout unreason, some ruthless creed
to a dozen dupes till dawn break.

"Every workday Eve fares
forth to the stores her foods to pluck,
while Adam hunts an easy dollar:
unperspiring at eventide
both eat their bread in boredom of spirit.

"The weekend comes that once was holy,
free still, but a feast no longer,
just time out, idiorhythmic,
when no ones cares what his neighbor does:
now newsprint and network are needed most.

"What they view may be vulgar rubbish,
what they listen to witless noise,
but it gives shelter, shields them from
Sunday's Bane, the basilisking
glare of Nothing, our pernicious foe.

4

"For what to Nothing shall nobodies answer?
Still super-physiques are socially there,
frequently photographed, feel at home,
but ordinary flesh is unwanted:
engines do better what biceps did.

"Quite soon computers may expel from the world
all but the top intelligent few,
the egos they leisure be left to dig
value and virtue from an invisible realm
of hobbies, sex, consumption, vague

"tussles with ghosts. Against Whom
shall the Sons band to rebel there,
where Troll-Father, Tusked-Mother,
are dream-monsters like dinosaurs
with a built-in obsolescence?

"A Gadgeted Age, but as unworldly
as when the faint light filtered down
on the first men in Mirkwood,
waiting their turn at the water hole
with the magic beasts who made the paths.

"Small marvel, then, if many adopt
cancer as the only offered career
worth while, if wards are full of
gents who believe they are Jesus Christ
or guilty of the Unforgivable Sin:

"if arcadian lawns where classic shoulders,
baroque bottoms, make *beaux gestes,*
is too tame a dream for the dislocated,

5

if their lewd fancies are of flesh debased
by damage, indignities, dirty words:

"if few now applaud a play that ends
   with warmth and pardon the word to all,
   as, blessed, unbamboozled, the bridal pairs,
   rustic and oppidan, in a ring-dance,
   image the stars at their stately bransles:

"if all has gone phut in the future we paint,
   where, vast and vacant, venomous areas
   surround the small sporadic patches
   of fen or forest that give food and shelter,
   such home as they have, to a human remnant,

"stunted in stature, strangely deformed,
   numbering by fives, with no zero,
   worshipping a ju-ju *General Mo*,
   in groups ruled by grandmothers,
   hirsute witches who on winter nights

"fable them stories of fair-haired Elves
   whose magic made the mountain dam,
   of Dwarves, cunning in craft, who smithied
   the treasure-hoards of tin cans?
   they flatten out for their hut roofs,

"nor choice they have nor change know,
   their fate ordained by fore-elders,
   the Oldest Ones, the wise spirits
   who through the mouths of masked wizards
   blessing give or blood demand.

6

"Still monied, immune, stands Megalopolis:
 happy he who hopes for better,
 what awaits Her may well be worse. . . ."

Thus I was thinking at three A.M.
 in mid-Manhattan till interrupted,
 cut short by a sharp voice.

"What fun and games you find it to play
 Jeremiah-cum-Juvenal:
 Shame on you for your *Schadenfreude.*"

"My!" I blustered, "how moral we're getting.
 A pococurante? Suppose I were,
 so what, if my words are true."

Thereupon, bored, a third voice:
"Go to sleep now for God's sake!
 You both will feel better by breakfast time."

Five Occasional Poems

JOSEPH WEINHEBER

(1892–1945)

Reaching my gate, a narrow
lane from the village
passes on into a wood:
when I walk that way
it seems befitting to stop
and look through the fence
of your garden where (under
the circs they had to)
they buried you like a loved
old family dog.

Categorized enemies
twenty years ago,
now next-door neighbors, we might
have become good friends,
sharing a common ambit
and love of the Word,
over a golden *Kremser*

had many a long
language on syntax, commas,
versification.

Yes, yes, it has to be said:
men of great damage
and malengine took you up.
Did they for long, though,
take you in, who to Goebbels'
offer of culture
countered—*in Ruah lossen?*
But Rag, Tag, Bobtail
prefer a stink, and the young
condemn you unread.

What, had you ever heard of
Franz Jägerstätter,
the St. Radegund peasant,
who said his lonely
Nein to the Aryan State
and was beheaded,
would your heart, as Austrian,
poet, have told you?
Good care, of course, was taken
you should hear nothing,

be unprepared for a day
that was bound to come,
a season of dread and tears
and dishevelment
when, transfixed by a nightmare,
you destroyed yourself.
Retribution was ever

9

a bungler at it:
dies alles ist furchtbar, hier
nur Schweigen gemäss.

Unmarked by me, unmourned for,
the hour of your death,
unhailed by you the moment
when, providence-led,
I first beheld Kirchstetten
on a pouring wet
October day in a year
that changed our cosmos,
the *annus mirabilis*
when Parity fell.

Already the realms that lost
were properly warm
and overeating, their crimes
the pedestrian
private sort, those nuisances,
corpses and rubble,
long carted away: for their raped
the shock was fading,
their kidnapped physicists felt
no longer homesick.

Today we smile at weddings
where bride and bridegroom
were both born since the Shadow
lifted, or rather
moved elsewhere: never as yet
has Earth been without
her bad patch, some unplace with

jobs for torturers
(In what bars are they welcome?
What girls marry them?),

or her nutritive surface
at peace all over.
No one, so far as we know,
has ever felt safe:
and so, in secret regions,
good family men
keep eye, devoted as monks,
on apparatus
inside which harmless matter
turns homicidal.

Here, though, I feel as at home
as you did: the same
short-lived creatures re-utter
the same carefree songs,
orchards cling to the regime
they know, from April's
rapid augment of color
till boisterous Fall,
when at each stammering gust
apples thump the ground.

Looking across our valley
where, hidden from view,
Sichelbach tottles westward
to join the Perchling,
humanely modest in scale
and mild in contour,
conscious of grander neighbors

to bow to, mountains
soaring behind me, ahead
a noble river,

I would respect you also,
Neighbor and Colleague,
for even my English ear
gets in your German
the workmanship and the note
of one who was graced
to hear the viols playing
on the impaled green,
committed thereafter *den
Abgrund zu nennen.*

EPITHALAMIUM

for PETER MUDFORD *and*
RITA AUDEN, *May 15, 1965*

All folk tales mean by ending
with a State Marriage,
feast and fireworks, we wish you,
Peter and Rita,
two idiosyncrasies
who opt in this hawthorn month
to common your lives.

A diffy undertaking,
for to us, whose dreams
are odorless, what is real
seems a bit smelly:
strong nerves are an advantage,
an accurate wristwatch too
can be a great help.

May Venus, to whose caprice
all blood must buxom,
take such a shine to you both

that, by her gifting,
your palpable substances
may re-ify those delights
they are purveyed for:

cool Hymen from Jealousy's
teratoid phantasms,
sulks, competitive headaches,
and Pride's monologue
that won't listen but demands
tautological echoes,
ever refrain you.

As genders, married or not,
who share with all flesh
a left-handed twist, your choice
reminds us to thank
Mrs. Nature for doing
(our ugly looks are our own)
the handsome by us.

For we're better built to last
than tigers, our skins
don't leak like the ciliates',
our ears can detect
quarter tones, even our most
myopic have good enough
vision for courtship:

and how uncanny it is
we're here to say so,
that life should have got to us
up through the City's
destruction layers after

surviving the inhuman
Permian purges.

Wherefore, as Mudfords, Audens,
Seth-Smiths, Bonnergees,
with civic spear and distaff
we hail a gangrel
Paleocene pseudo-rat,
the Ur-Papa of princes
and crossing-sweepers:

as Adams, Eves, commanded
to nonesuch being,
answer the One for Whom all
enantiomorphs
are super-posable, yet
Who numbers each particle
by its Proper Name.

EULOGY

for PROFESSOR NEVILL COGHILL
on the occasion of his retirement in 1966

In our beginning
was a snuffling life without
sky or horizon,
full of objects and not-theres,
too close, over-big,
and not all of them friendly,
lit up at moments
from an invisible source
by shafts of sunlight
or a split-second levin:
childhood remembered
as a row of cloudless days
is a revision

we make later on,
after we've learned from noting
the habits of stars
to annal births, bereavements,
manage dimensions

16

with standard weights and measures,
derive our rages
into useful leats, and know,
without knowing when,
we've made our bed. Whoever
is waiting for us
at ford or crossroads cannot
be avoided now:

and we must pray for
a good death, whatever
world we are destined
to look on last. It could be
a field of battle,
or a vista of terse lawns
and tantalized yews,
or a forgotten province
of sagging fences,
weeds and pecker-wood sawmills,
where an ill-nourished
sullen people vegetate
in some gloomy schism.

But Then was also
an Age of Care: what Nature
was doing to us
had to be coped with, the frown
of crag or cupboard
no more to be laughed away
than a Cruel Fair,
wife-trouble, debts, or public
crises when the State
trots out its Higher Clergy.
Between, though, with luck,

for a columbine season
we are free to play,

swains of a pasture
where neither love nor money
nor clocks are cogent,
a time to wear odd clothing,
behave with panache
and talk nonsense as I did,
ambling in Oxford's
potamic meadows with friends:
one austere dogma
capped another, abstract noun
echoed abstract noun,
to voice our irreverent
amoebean song.

Blessed be Christ Church
for having been so snooty
forty years ago
about E. Lit. (What reason
had I to suppose
Exeter worth a visit?):
now of the body
I brashly came to my first
tutorial in
not a molecule remains,
but to its mind's eye
optically definite
is our meeting still.

This Nevill, I knew,
was not a *Heldentenor*
of the lecture hall,

not a disciple-hunting
Socratic bully,
not a celibate glutton
averse to pupils
as to mal-edited texts,
yet a don distinct
as these from the common plump,
and as a Privy
Councillor more deserving
of our vail and verge.

Endowed with the charm
of your Irish provenance
but no proper-false,
you countenanced all species,
the alphas, the bone-
-idle, the obstreperous
and the really rum,
never looked cross or sleepy
when our essays were
more about us than Chaucer,
and no unfinished
shy production felt afraid
to knock on your door.

Among the aging
too large a group disappoint
by looking a mess,
and even Aphrodite's
ex-darlings who once
swanned through crowds, the stare of all,
turn lipless vipers
or red-nosed stertorous bores,
but you have induced

your structure of carbon-rings
and brine to assume
a face that features a self
serene yet haggard,

a life lived droitly,
with a license from now on
for any conduct
in mild Gloucestershire, whither
our love shall follow:
may sunbeams, falling across
your breakfast table,
forecast new agreeable hours
to paint in, rethumb
a pet author, night by night
through your dreams the sound
of lapsing brooks assure you
that you pass muster.

ELEGY

IN MEMORIAM EMMA EIERMANN
ob. November 4, 1967

Liebe Frau Emma,
na, was hast Du denn gemacht?
You who always made
such conscience of our comfort,
oh, how could you go and die,

as if you didn't know
that in a permissive age
so rife with envy,
a housekeeper is harder
to replace than a lover,

and die, too, when we
were thousands of miles away,
leaving no one there
to prune and transplant before
the winter cold should set in.

Good witch that you were,
surely you should have foreseen

the doom that your death
would spell for your cats and ours:
all had to be put away.

You came with the house,
you and your brother Josef,
Sudetendeutsche
made homeless paupers when Czechs
got their turn to be brutal:

but catastrophe
had failed to modernize you,
Child of the Old World,
in which to serve a master
was never thought ignoble.

Children of the New,
we had to learn how to live
in the older way,
well tendered and observed by
loyal but critical eyes.

From the first, I think,
you liked us, but to the last
assumed most callers
knocked with some evil intent
(now and again you were right).

When guests were coming,
there was always the worry:—
would you disallow?
Greeks, in your censure, were rogues,
all teen-agers delinquent.

Nor were you ever
one to behave your temper:
let Youth pick a fruit
or flower, out you would storm,
arms whirling, screaming abuse

in peasant German
at startled Americans
who had meant no harm,
and, after they'd gone, for days
you would treat us to the sulks.

But when in good form,
how enchanting your shy grin,
your soft cat-language:
no, no, Frau E, dear oddling,
we shall always be grateful.

After Josef died
(siblings can live in a bond
as close as wedlock),
you were all amort, your one
wish to rejoin him quickly.

You have, and we're left
with ten years to consider,
astonished at how
vivid they are to recall:
Du gute, schlaf in Ruhe.

A MOSAIC
FOR MARIANNE MOORE

ON THE OCCASION OF HER EIGHTIETH BIRTHDAY,
November 15, 1967

The concluded gardens of personal liking   *beautiful live*
are enchanted habitats
where real toads may catch imaginary flies
and the climate will accommodate the tiger
and the polar bear.

So in the middle of yours (where it is human
to sit) we see you sitting
in a wide-brimmed hat beneath a monkey-puzzle,
at your feet the beasts you animated for us
by thinking of them.

Your lion with ferocious chrysanthemum head,
your jerboa, erect on
his Chippendale claw, your pelican behaving
like charred paper, your musk-ox who smells of water,
your fond nautilus,

cope with what surprises them and greet the stranger
in a Midwestern accent,

24

even that bum, the unelephantine creature
who is certainly here to worship and often
selected to mourn.

Egocentric, eccentric, he will name a cat
Peter, a new car *Edsel,*
emphasize his own birthday and a few others
he thinks deserve it, as today we stress your name,
Miss Marianne Moore

who, fastidious but fair, are unaffronted
by those whose disposition
it is to affront, who beg the cobra's pardon,
are always on time and never would yourself write
error with four *r*'s.

For poems, dolphin-graceful as carts from Sweden,
our thank-you should be a right
good salvo of barks: it's much too muffled to say
"how well and with what unfreckled integrity
it has all been done."

The Horatians

Into what fictive realms can imagination
translate you, Flaccus, and your kin? Not the courts of
    Grand Opera, that *galère*
    of lunatics, power-famished

or love-ravenous, belting out their arias,
nor the wards of *Buffa,* either, where abnormal
    growths of self-love are excised
    by the crude surgery of a

practical joke. Perhaps the only invented
story in which your appearance seems credible
    is the Whodunit: I can
    believe in one of you solving

a murder which has the professionals baffled,
thanks to your knowledge of local topography.
    In our world all of you share
    a love for some particular

place and stretch of country, a farm near Tivoli
or a Radnorshire village: what the Capital
    holds out as a lure, a chance
    to get into Society,

does not tempt you, who wry from crowds, traffic-noises,
bluestockings and millionaires. Your tastes run to
    small dinner parties, small rooms,
    and the tone of voice that suits them,

neither truckle nor thrasonical but softly
certain (a sound wood-winds imitate better
    than strings), your most worldly wish
    a genteel sufficiency of

land or lolly. Among those I really know, the
British branch of the family, how many have
    found in the Anglican Church
    your Maecenas who enabled

a life without cumber, as pastors adjective
to rustic flocks, as organists in trollopish
    cathedral towns. Then, in all
    labyrinthine economies

there are obscure nooks into which Authority
never pokes a suspicious nose, *embusqué* havens
    for natural bachelors
    and political idiots,

Zoological and Botanical Gardens,
museum basements displaying feudal armor
    or old coins: there, too, we find
    you among the custodians.

Some of you have written poems, usually
short ones, and some kept diaries, seldom published
    till after your deaths, but most
    make no memorable impact

except on your friends and dogs. Enthusiastic
Youth writes you off as cold, who cannot be found on
    barricades, and never shoot
    either yourselves or your lovers.

You thought well of your Odes, Flaccus, and believed they
would live, but knew, and have taught your descendants to
    say with you: "As makers go,
    compared with Pindar or any

of the great foudroyant masters who don't ever
amend, we are, for all our polish, of little
    stature, and, as human lives,
    compared with authentic martyrs

like Regulus, of no account. We can only
do what it seems to us we were made for, look at
    this world with a happy eye
    but from a sober perspective."

Profile

He thanks God daily
that he was born and bred
a British Pharisee.

$*$ $*$ $*$

A childhood full of love
and good things to eat:
why should he not hate change?

$*$ $*$ $*$

Gluttony and Sloth
have often protected him
from Lust and Anger.

$*$ $*$ $*$

In his cups neither savage nor maudlin,
but all too prone
to hold forth.

$*$ $*$ $*$

Too timid to cruise,
in his feudal daydream no
courage is needed.
The Cardinal halts his coach:
"Dear Child, you please me. Hop in!"

* * *

The way he dresses
reveals an angry baby,
howling to be dressed.

* * *

He has often stamped his feet,
wept on occasion,
but never been bored.

* * *

Vain? Not very, except
about his knowledge of metre,
and his friends.

* * *

Praise? Unimportant,
but jolly to remember
while falling asleep.

* * *

He likes giving presents,
but finds it hard to forget
what each one cost.

* * *

He envies those who have learned,
when reading newspapers.
how to fold them.

* * *

He wishes he were
Konrad Lorenz and had written
Firbank's novels.

* * *

Reaching a crossroads,
he expects the traffic lights
to turn green for him.

* * *

So obsessive a ritualist
a pleasant surprise
makes him cross.

* * *

Without a watch
he would never know when
to feel hungry or horny.

* * *

His guardian angel
has always told him
What and Whom to read next.

* * *

Conscious of his good luck,
he wonders why so few
people kill themselves.

* * *

Scanning his fellow
Subway passengers, he asks:
"Can I really be
the only one in this car
who is glad to be alive?"

* * *

On waking, he thinks:
"Precious, Precious Me!
A fig for your detractors!"

On going to bed:
"What *am* I to do?
Again You have let Us down."

Since

On a mid-December day,
frying sausages
for myself, I abruptly
felt under fingers
thirty years younger the rim
of a steering wheel,
on my cheek the parching wind
of an August noon,
as passenger beside me
You as then you were.

Slap across a veg-growing
alluvial plain
we raced in clouds of white dust,
and geese fled screaming
as we missed them by inches,
making a beeline
for mountains gradually
enlarging eastward,

joyfully certain nightfall
would occasion joy.

It did. In a flagged kitchen
we were served broiled trout
and a rank cheese: for a while
we talked by the fire,
then, carrying candles, climbed
steep stairs. Love was made
then and there: so halcyoned,
soon we fell asleep
to the sound of a river
swabbling through a gorge.

Since then, other enchantments
have blazed and faded,
enemies changed their address,
and War made ugly
an uncountable number
of unknown neighbors,
precious as us to themselves:
but round your image
there is no fog, and the Earth
can still astonish.

Of what, then, should I complain,
pottering about
a neat suburban kitchen?
Solitude? Rubbish!
It's social enough with real
faces and landscapes
for whose friendly countenance
I at least can learn
to live with obesity
and a little fame.

34

Amor Loci

I could draw its map by heart,
showing its contours,
strata and vegetation,
name every height,
small burn and lonely shieling,
but nameless to me,
faceless as heather or grouse,
are those who live there,

its dead too vague for judgment,
tangible only
what they wrought, their giant works
of delve and drainage
in days preterite: long since
their hammering stopped
as the lodes all petered out
in the Jew Limestone.

Here and there a tough chimney
still towers over

dejected masonry, moss,
decomposed machines,
with no one about, no chance
of buttering bread,
a land postured in my time
for marginal farms.

Any musical future
is most unlikely.
Industry wants Cheap Power,
romantic muscle
a perilous wilderness,
Mr. Pleasure pays
for surf-riding, claret, sex:
it offers them none.

To me, though, much: a vision,
not (as perhaps at
twelve I thought it) of Eden,
still less of a New
Jerusalem but, for one,
convinced he will die,
more comely, more credible
than either daydream.

How, but with some real focus
of desolation
could I, by analogy,
imagine a love
that, however often smeared,
Shrugged at, abandoned
by a frivolous worldling,
does not abandon?

Metaphor

Nose, I am free
To turn up or thumb
At my neighbor, stick into
His business, it's You,
Also, through Whom
For my liberties he
With like insolence may
Make me pay.

Bird-Language

Trying to understand the words
    Uttered on all sides by birds,
I recognize in what I hear
    Noises that betoken fear.

Though some of them, I'm certain, must
    Stand for rage, bravado, lust,
All other notes that birds employ
    Sound like synonyms for joy.

Two Songs

I

SONG OF THE OGRES

Little fellow, you're amusing,
Stop before you end by losing
    Your shirt:
Run along to Mother, Gus,
Those who interfere with us
    Get hurt.

Honest Virtue, old wives prattle,
Always wins the final battle.
    Dear, Dear!
Life's exactly what it looks,
Love may triumph in the books,
    Not here.

We're not joking, we assure you:
Those who rode this way before you
    Died hard.
What? Still spoiling for a fight?
Well, you've asked for it alright:
    On guard!

Always hopeful, aren't you? Don't be.
Night is falling and it won't be
    Long now:
You will never see the dawn,
You will wish you'd not been born.
    And how!

II

SONG OF THE DEVIL

Ever since observation taught me temptation
Is a matter of timing, I've tried
To clothe my fiction in up-to-date diction,
The contemporary jargon of Pride.
    I can recall when, to win the more
      Obstinate round,
    The best bet was to say to them: "Sin the more
      That Grace may abound."

Since Social Psychology replaced Theology
The process goes twice as quick,
If a conscience is tender and loth to surrender
I have only to whisper: "You're sick!
    Puritanical morality
      Is madly Non-U:
    Enhance your personality
      With a Romance, with two.

"If you pass up a dame, you've yourself to blame,
For shame is neurotic, so snatch!
All rules are too formal, in fact they're abnormal,

For any desire is natch.
        So take your proper share, man, of
            Dope and drink:
        Aren't you the Chairman of
            Ego, Inc.?

"Free-Will is a mystical myth as statistical
Methods have objectively shown,
A fad of the Churches: since the latest researches
Into Motivation it's known
        That Honor is hypocrisy,
            Honesty a joke.
        You live in a Democracy:
            Lie like other folk.

"Since men are like goods, what are shouldn'ts or shoulds
When you are the Leading Brand?
Let them all drop dead, you're way ahead,
Beat them up if they dare to demand
        What may your intention be,
            Or what might ensue:
        There's a difference of dimension be-
            -tween the rest and you.

"If in the scrimmage of business your image
Should ever tarnish or stale,
Public Relations can take it and make it
Shine like a Knight of the Grail.
        You can mark up the price that you sell at, if
            Your package has glamour and show:
        Values are relative.
            Dough is dough.

"So let each while you may think you're more O.K.,
More yourself than anyone else,
Till you find that you're hooked, your goose is cooked,
And you're only a cipher of Hell's.
        Believe while you can that I'm proud of you,
            Enjoy your dream:
        I'm so bored with the whole fucking crowd of you
            I could *scream!*"

Forty Years On

Except where blast-furnaces and generating-stations
    have inserted their sharp profiles,
or a Thruway slashes harshly across them, Bohemia's contours
    look just as amiable now
as when I saw them first (indeed, her coast is gentler,
    for tame hotels have ousted
the havocking bears), nor have her dishes lost their flavor
    since Florizel was thwacked into exile
and we and Sicily discorded, fused into rival amalgams,
    in creed and policy oppugnant.
Only to the ear is it patent something drastic has happened,
    that orators no more speak
of primogeniture, prerogatives of age and sceptre:
    (for our health we have had to learn
the fraternal shop of our new Bonzen, but that was easy).
    For a useful technician I lacked
the schooling, for a bureaucrat the *Sitzfleisch:* all I had
    was the courtier's agility to adapt
my rogueries to the times. It sufficed. I survived and prosper

better than I ever did under
the old lackadaisical economy: it is many years now
      since I picked a pocket (how deft
my hand was then!), or sang for pennies, or traveled on foot.
      (The singing I miss, but today's
audience would boo my ballads: it calls for Songs of Protest
      and wants its bawdry straight
not surreptitious.) A pedlar still, for obvious reasons
      I no longer cry my wares,
but in ill-lit alleys coaxingly whisper to likely clients:

      Anything you cannot buy
      In the stores I will supply,
      English footwear, nylon hose,
      Or transistor radios;
      Come to me for the Swiss Francs
      Unobtainable in banks;
      For a price I can invent
      Any official document,
      Work Permits, Driving Licenses,
      Any Certificate you please:
      Believe me, I know all the tricks,
      There is nothing I can't fix.

      Why, then, should I badger?
No rheum has altered my gait, as ever my cardiac muscles
      are undismayed, my cells
perfectly competent, and by now I am far too rich
      for the thought of the hangman's noose
to make me oggle. But how glib all the faces I see about me
      seem suddenly to have become,
and how seldom I feel like a hay-tumble. For three nights running
      now I have had the same dream
of a suave afternoon in Fall. I am standing on high ground,
      looking out westward over
a plain run smoothly by Jaguar farmers. In the eloignment,

a-glitter in the whelking sun,
a sheer bare cliff concludes the vista. At its base I see,
    black, shaped like a bell-tent,
the mouth of a cave by which (I know in my dream) I am to
    make my final exit,
its roof so low it will need an awkward duck to make it.
    "Well, will that be so shaming?"
I ask when awake. Why should it be? When has Autolycus
    ever solemned himself?

Marginalia

I

Fate succumbs
many a species: one alone
jeopardizes itself.

∗ ∗ ∗

The gregarious
and mild-tempered never know
each other by name:
creatures who make friends are shy
and liable to anger.

∗ ∗ ∗

Unable to see
a neighbor to frown at,
Eutroplus beat his wife.

(after Konrad Lorenz)

∗ ∗ ∗

46

Afraid or ashamed to say
I don't like you,
he yawned and scratched himself.

* * *

The palm extended in welcome:
Look! for you
I have unclenched my fist.

* * *

Afraid after long
separation of meeting
a hostile stranger,
the two old friends reaffirmed
their pact with peals of laughter.

* * *

Brashly triumphant,
overdogmatic, a sneeze
asserts without proof
some ritual connection
between breathing and loving.

* * *

Born with high voices
and first responding to one,
even as basses
we feel an operatic
hero must be a tenor.

* * *

Few can remember
clearly when innocence came

47

to a sudden end,
the moment at which we ask
for the first time: *Am I loved?*

* * *

Fear and Vanity
incline us to imagine
we have caused a face
to turn away which merely
happened to look somewhere else.
                    (after Erik Erikson)

* * *

Everyone thinks:
"I am the most important
Person at present."
The sane remember to add:
"Important, I mean, to me."

* * *

Wooziness that knows it is woozy
may tell truths
Logic is deaf to.

* * *

True Love enjoys
twenty-twenty vision,
but talks like a myopic.

* * *

Justice: permission to peck
a wee bit harder
than we have been pecked.

* * *

48

The introvert is deaf
to his neighbor's cry
at the extrovert's pinch.

* * *

Needing above all
silence and warmth, we produce
brutal cold and noise.

* * *

Wicked deeds have their glamour,
but those who commit them
are always bores.

* * *

When we do evil,
we and our victims
are equally bewildered.

* * *

The decent, probably,
outnumber the swine,
but few can inherit

the genes, or procure
both the money and time,
to join the civilized.

II

A dead man
who never caused others to die
seldom rates a statue.

* * *

The last king
of a fallen dynasty
is seldom well spoken of.

* * *

Few even wish they could read
the lost annals
of a cudgeled people.

* * *

The tyrant's device:
*Whatever Is Possible
Is Necessary.*

* * *

Small tyrants, threatened by big,
sincerely believe
they love Liberty.

* * *

No tyrant ever fears
his geologists or his engineers.

* * *

Tyrants may get slain,
but their hangmen usually
die in their beds.

* * *

Patriots? Little boys,
obsessed by Bigness,
Big Pricks, Big Money, Big Bangs.

* * *

In States unable
to alleviate Distress,
Discontent is hanged.

* * *

In semiliterate countries
demagogues pay
court to teen-agers.

* * *

When Chiefs of State
prefer to work at night,
let the citizens beware.

III

Ancestorless,
the upstart warrior proclaimed
the Sun his Father.

$$* \quad * \quad *$$

Their gods:—like themselves
greedy skirt-chasing blackguards
without compunction,
but (as, thank God, they were not)
forever young and intact.

$$* \quad * \quad *$$

On their stage swords, horses
were sacred persons, the poor
farting bumpkins.

$$* \quad * \quad *$$

Wars, revolts, plagues, inflation:
no wonder they dreamed of God

as a Logical
One, for Whom to be solid
or moved was vulgar.

$* \quad * \quad *$

He praised his God
for the expertise
of his torturer and his chef.

$* \quad * \quad *$

Voracious eater,
shrewd diplomat though he was,
when playing checkers
he forgot about meal times,
kept ambassadors waiting.

$* \quad * \quad *$

While the Empire went to pot,
he amused himself
extemporizing moral,
highly moral, iambics,
deficient in rhythm.

$* \quad * \quad *$

A neglected wife,
she refused to mope, but filled
her lonely bedroom
with costly apparatus
for distilling new perfumes:

had made to order
a metal icon of Christ
which answered questions
and foretold future events

53

by a change in its colors.

(after Psellus)

* * *

With silver mines,
recruiting grounds,
a general of real genius,

he thought himself invulnerable:
in one battle
he lost all three.

* * *

After the massacre
they pacified their conscience
by telling jokes.

* * *

Reluctant at first
to break his sworn promise
of Safe Conduct, after

consulting his confessor,
in good spirits
he signed a death warrant.

* * *

Be godly, he told his flock,
*bloody and extreme
like the Holy Ghost.*

* * *

When their Infidel
Paymaster fell in arrears,

the mercenaries
recalled their unstained childhoods
in devout Christian homes.

* * *

After the Just War,
the Holy War that had saved
Christendom, there were
more palaces and clergy,
fewer scholars and houses.

(after Ilsa Barea)

* * *

The Huguenot church bells
were flogged, then baptized
as Roman Catholics.

(after Friedrich Heer)

* * *

The Queen fled, leaving
books behind her
that shocked the pious usurper.

* * *

Intelligent, rich,
humane, the young man dreamed of
posthumous glory
as connoisseur and patron
of Scholarship and the Arts.

An age bent on war,
the ambitions of his king,
decreed otherwise:

55

he was to be remembered
as a destroyer of towns.

* * *

Born to flirt and write light verses,
he died bravely
by the headsman's axe.

* * *

Into the prosperous quiet
between two wars
came *Anopheles*.

* * *

Under a Sovereign
who despised culture
Arts and Letters improved.

* * *

Wartime. English schoolboys
killing the white butterflies
they called Frenchmen.

* * *

Rumors ran through the city
that the Tsar's bodyguard
was not house-trained.

* * *

Assembling
with ceremonial pomp,
the Imperial Diet

gravely debated
legislation
it had no power to reject.

* * *

He hid when he saw
a Minister approaching
with a worried look.

* * *

In the intervals between
bathing and tennis
he sought new allies.

* * *

Ready any day
to pistol each other
on a point of honor,

night after night
they staked their fortunes, knowing
there were money-lenders

they could always cheat
by absconding to Dieppe
or shooting themselves.

* * *

The tobacco farmers
were Baptists who considered
smoking a sin.

* * *

Abandoning his wives,
he fled with their jewels
and two hundred dogs.

* * *

To maintain a stud
of polo-ponies he now
was too stout to ride,
he slapped taxes on windows,
hearthstones and doorsteps and wives.

* * *

He walked like someone
who'd never had to
open a door for himself.

* * *

Victorious over
the foreign tyrant,
the patriots retained

his emergency
police regulations,
devised to suppress them.

* * *

Providentially
right for once in his lifetime
(his reasons were wrong),
the old sod was permitted
to save civilization.

IV

Animals femurs,
ascribed to saints who never
existed, are still

more holy than portraits
of conquerors who,
unfortunately, did.

* * *

Like any Zola
they poked their noses into
prisons and brothels,
not, though, in search of copy
but to comfort their equals.

* * *

To shock pagan purists
he never avoided
a metacismus.

* * *

With equal affection
he bathed the sick
and studied Greek papyri.

* * *

The young scamp turned into
a hermit, renowned for
his way with vipers.

* * *

A choleric type,
he was always butting in
to defend the Jews
against the mob, or the poor
against the King's warreners.

* * *

Knowing that God knew
that what she really liked best
was not the stable
but the crowded inn, she built
a fine hospice for pilgrims.

* * *

Getting up to pray
in the middle of the night,
she told her husband
(a heathen and a bad hat):
I must go to the bathroom.

* * *

On his return from foreign parts
where he had suffered
and learned mercy,

he abrogated at once
the Penal Code
his knavish gamekeeper,

his ignorant housemaids,
had enacted against
innocent barn owls.

(after Charles Waterton)

* * *

Who died in Nineteen-Sixty-Five
more worthy of honors
than *Lark,* a cow

who gave to mankind
one-hundred-and-fifteen-thousand
litres of milk?

V

Once having shat
in his new apartment,
he began to feel at home.

∗ ∗ ∗

Another entire day wasted.
What is called for?
The Whip? Pills? Patience?

∗ ∗ ∗

His thoughts pottered
from verses to sex to God
without punctuation.

∗ ∗ ∗

Mulberries dropping,
twinges of lumbago,
as he read *Clarendon.*

∗ ∗ ∗

Round the ritual bonfire
on Midsummer Eve
another generation,
who never walk, drink no wine,
carry transistors.

* * *

A September night:
just the two of them, eating
corn from their garden,
plucked thirty minutes ago.
Outside: thunder, siling rain.

* * *

On the bushes
St. Martin's gossamer,
in the bathroom a stray toad.

* * *

Leaf-fall. A lane. A rogue,
driving to visit
someone who still trusts him.

* * *

Imaged in the bar-mirror
during their lunch hour,
a row of city faces,
middle-aged, mute, expecting
no death of their own.

* * *

How cheerful they looked,
the unoccupied bar stools

in mid-afternoon,
freed for some hours from the weight
of drab defeated bottoms.

* * *

How could he help him?
miserable youth! in flight
from a non-father,
an incoherent mother,
in pursuit of—what?

* * *

The Marquis de Sade and Genet
Are highly thought of today,
    But torture and treachery
    Are not his kinds of lechery,
So he's given his copies away.

* * *

Americans—like omelets:
there is no such thing
as a pretty good one.

* * *

Even Hate should be precise:
very few White Folks
have fucked their mothers.

* * *

As a Wasp, riding
the Subway, he wonders why
it is that nearly

all the aristocratic
faces he sees are Negro.

* * *

Passing Beauty
still delights him, but he no longer
has to turn round.

* * *

Post coitum homo tristis.
What nonsense! If he could,
he would sing.

* * *

Listening to the *Études*
of Chopin, entranced
by such a love-match of Craft
and Utterance, he forgot
his Love was not there.

* * *

Lonely he may be
but, each time he bolts his door
the last thing at night,
his heart rejoices: "No one
can interfere with me now."

* * *

He woke in the small hours,
dismayed by a wilderness
of hostile thoughts.

* * *

The shame in aging
is not that Desire should fail
(Who mourns for something
he no longer needs?) : it is
that someone else must be told.

* * *

Thoughts of his own death,
like the distant roll
of thunder at a picnic.

* * *

Pulling on his socks,
he recalls that his grand-pa
went pop in the act.

* * *

How odd it now seems
that, when he was born, there seemed
nothing odd about writing:
*I traveled alone
to Bonn with a boring maid.*

* * *

Years before doctors
had invented the jargon,
he knew from watching
his maiden aunts that illness
could be psychosomatic.

* * *

Father at the wars,
Mother, tongue-tied with shyness,

struggling to tell him
the Facts of Life he dared not
tell her he knew already.

∗ ∗ ∗

The class whose vices
he pilloried was his own,
now extinct, except
for lone survivors like him
who remember its virtues.

Eight Songs from *Mother Courage*

(German text by Berthold Brecht. Music by Paul Dessau)

MOTHER COURAGE'S SONG

Scene I

Good Captain, bid the drums be silent,
Your weary marchers stand at ease:
Here comes their old friend Mother Courage
With things to sell that ought to please.
I've good strong boots, I've warm thick woolens,
And every sort of useful gear,
For even lousy cannon-fodder
Should have at least good boots to wear.

Before you give them marching orders,
Good Captain, let your soldiers buy:
Let Mother Courage first refresh them
With food and drink before they die.
For cannon on an empty stomach,
That's not so good, as you know well:
They've had enough, but take my blessing,
Then drive them through the jaws of Hell.

68

The snow has gone. Good souls, arise!
The dead lie still. They can't obey,
When those who still have legs and eyes
Lace up their boots and march away.

Scene VII

When courage fails, when hopes are fading,
Think on the victory ahead,
For war is but a kind of trading:
Instead of cheese, it deals in lead.

Some have done deeds they took a pride in,
Some slyly sought their lives to save:
With care they dug a hole to hide in,
But merely dug an early grave.

How many brave fire, hail and thunder,
In hope to reach a quiet shore,
Who, when they get there, only wonder
Exactly what they braved them for.

Scene VIII

From Ulm to Metz, Metz to Moravia,
Still Mother Courage will be there
With lots of lead and loads of powder:
The war provides substantial fare.

War cannot live on bullets only,
Nor powder either: it needs men.
Unless you flock to join the colors,
It can't go on: so, join up then!

Choral Finale

With blood and fire, with vain endeavor,
To other lands the war has gone:
The war goes on and on forever,
And what have we to count upon?
Some shit, some grub, a skirt, some plunder,
And stolen pay we'll never get,
Tomorrow, though, may see a wonder:
The campaign is not ended yet.

The snow has gone. Good souls, arise!
The dead lie still. They can't obey,
When those who still have legs and eyes
Lace up their boots and march away.

SONG OF THE GOOD WIFE
AND THE INVADERS

Your cannon may blab and your sabers may jab,
But the river will grab you rash waders:
O take my advice, beware of the ice!
Cried the goodwife to the invaders.

When cannons pound and the orders go round,
Hearing the drum-beat, we laugh at the sound,
No danger has ever dismayed us.
So away! Whether southward, whether northward we're bound,
With a saber in hand we will stand our ground.
Answered the marching invaders.

Ah, watch what you do! What I tell you is true.
For the sake of the good God who made us,
O believe what I say: your death lies that way.
Cried the goodwife to the invaders.

Balls! they all roared, waved a lance or a sword,
Laughed aloud in her face and marched down to the ford.

No river has ever delayed us,
And when down on your rooftop the full moon whitely stares,
There'll be feasting and fun. Think of that in your prayers!
Answered the marching invaders.

Life is quickly snuffed out; like a stove it goes out,
And your deeds will be nothing to aid us.
Ah, how quick dries the dew! May God save me and you!
Cried the goodwife to the invaders.

Then every soldier with lance or with sword
Stormed into the stream, was soon grabbed by the ford,
And its waters ate up all the stormers.
Every life was snuffed out: all our stoves have gone out,
And their deeds can do nothing to warm us.

SONG OF FRATERNIZATION

I remember I was just seventeen
When the foe invaded our land:
With a smile he laid aside his saber,
And with a smile he gave me his hand.
That May the days were bright,
And starry every night.
The regiment stood on parade:
They gave their drums the usual thwack,
They led us then behind a stack,
Where they fraternized with us.

Our foes were strong and many,
An army-cook was mine:
I hated my foe by daylight.
But, O, I loved him by moonshine.
Now all the days are bright,
And starry every night.
The regiment stands on parade:
They give their drums the usual thwack,

73

Again, again, behind a stack,
There they fraternize with us.

Such a love must come from Heaven,
It was the will of Fate:
The others could never understand me,
How I could love where I should hate.
Then came a rainy morn,
A day of grief and scorn.
The regiment stood on parade:
The drums beat as they always do.
There stood my foe, my darling too;
Then they marched away from us.

SONG OF UNCONDITIONAL SURRENDER

In the long ago I was just like all of you,
Thought myself the most important girl in town,
Someone special, ordered soup without a hair in it:
None, I said, shall ever get me down.
But a bird sang clear: "Tweet! Wait a year.
For into church you soon shall go,
Walking quick or walking slow,
And on your little trumpet blow.
Soon he'll be here."
Some are in luck: some not.
Man may propose, but God disposes.
If He does, so what!

The days went by and before that year was done
I'd learned how girls must take their medicine every night,
For by the time they were well and truly through with me,
You can bet they had me on my arse and knees alright.
Yet a bird sang clear: "Tweet! Not this year.
Now into church the soldiers go,

Marching quick or marching slow,
And on their little trumpets blow.
Soon he'll be here."
Some are in luck: some not.
Man may propose, but God disposes.
If He does, so what!

I've heard many say: "Heaven shall obey my will,
And no star is big or bright enough for me."
But they soon found, all day piling rocky hill on rocky hill,
What a weight a straw hat even comes to be.
Still a bird sings clear: "Tweet! Wait a year.
Then into church you both shall go,
Walking quick or walking slow,
And on your little trumpets blow.
Soon he'll be here."
Some are in luck: some not.
Man may propose, but God disposes.
If He does, so what!

SONG OF THE SOLDIER
BEFORE THE INN

A drink, man, quick! It's a crime.
The cavalry have no time,
Fighting for King and Country.

Your breast, girl, quick! It's a crime.
The cavalry have no time,
Riding for King and Country.

Your bid, mate, quick! It's a crime.
We cavalry have no time,
Must follow the flag of our Country.

No sermon, now, Rev! It's a crime.
The cavalry have no time,
Dying for King and Country.

SONG OF THE ROSE

The red garden rose we planted
Has fair and stately grown;
Our fondest hopes were granted.
Scarlet heavy-scented flowers
Beguiled our summer hours:
Blessed those are who a garden own
Where such a rose-tree flowers.

Though, through the pine woods wailing,
The winter wind makes moan,
Its rage is unavailing.
Long before the autumn ended,
Our roof with tiles we mended:
Blessed those are who a roof still own
When such a wind comes wailing.

LULLABY

Hush-a-bye, Baby, sleep for a while;
Others' brats whimper, but mine only smile:
Wet straw their pillows, but you lie on down
And silk soft as an angel's evening gown.
They get a dry crust, but you shall have cake
And warm milk to refresh you whenever you wake.
Hush-a-bye, Baby, sleep without care:
One baby lies in Poland, the other is who knows where.

SONG OF THE TRIALS
OF GREAT SOULS

Upon his throne sat Solomon,
The greatest king on earth;
No man was half so wise as he.
"Cursed," he cried, "be the day and hour of my birth,
For life and works are vanity."
How great and wise was Solomon,
Who only longed for night to fall.
Then worldly men this moral drew:
If that is what his wisdom has brought him to,
How blessed is he with none at all.

What courage Julius Caesar had,
A warrior without peer,
In look and bearing how sublime,
But with daggers they slew him just at the time
He'd reached the height of his career.
He gave one cry—"You, Brutus, too!"—
Before he fell, as night must fall.
Then worldly men this moral drew:

If that is what his courage has brought him to,
How blessed is he with none at all.

How golden-tongued was Socrates,
Who always spoke the truth,
But high-ups do not like to think:
As a scorner of gods, corrupter of youth,
The hemlock cup he had to drink.
The light of all the Greeks was he,
But shone in vain, for night must fall.
Then worldly men this moral drew:
If that is what his logic has brought him to,
How blessed is he with none at all.

St. Martin met a poor old man,
As holy legend saith:
The winter wind was chill and grim,
So one half of his cloak the saint gave to him,
And soon enough both froze to death.
On earth the saint sought no reward,
But earth is earth where night must fall.
Then worldly man this moral drew:
If that is what his charity brought him to,
How blessed is he with none at all.

There're Ten Commandments unto which
All proper folk pay heed,
But which of them has helped a bit?
You who by fireside or stove may cozily sit,
Remember those in care and need.
How honest we were, through and through,
But times have changed and night must fall.
Then worldly men this moral drew:
If that is what religion has brought us to,
How blessed is he with none at all.

In Due Season

Springtime, Summer and Fall: days to behold a world
Antecedent to our knowing, where flowers think
Theirs concretely in scent-colors and beasts, the same
Age all over, pursue dumb horizontal lives
On one level of conduct and so cannot be
Secretary to man's plot to become divine.

Lodged in all is a set metronome: thus, in May
Bird-babes still in the egg click to each other *Hatch!;*
June-struck cuckoos go off-pitch; when obese July
Turns earth's heating up, unknotting their poisoned ropes,
Vipers move into play; warned by October's nip,
Younger leaves to the old give the releasing draught.

Winter, though, has the right tense for a look indoors
At ourselves, and with First Names to sit face-to-face,
Time for reading of thoughts, time for the trying-out
Of new metres and new recipes, proper time
To reflect on events noted in warmer months
Till, transmuted, they take part in a human tale.

82

There, responding to our cry for intelligence,
Nature's mask is relaxed into a mobile grin,
Stones, old shoes, come alive, born sacramental signs,
Nod to us in the First Person of mysteries
They know nothing about, bearing a message from
The invisible sole Source of specific things.

Rois Fainéants

On High Feast-Days they were given a public airing:
Their shoulder-length blond hair combed and braided,
In carts drawn by white oxen they were paraded
Before the eyes of the people, children bearing
The names of fabulous ancestors, Chlotar, Chilperic,
Clovis, Théodoric, Dagobert, Childeric,
In whose veins ran the royal blood, declared descended
In unbroken line (the facts were sometimes amended)
From sea-gods or sea-monsters of old, on which succession
The luck of the Franks, though now Catholic, still depended.
Everyone knew, of course, it was a staged play,
Everyone knew where the real power lay,
That it was the Mayor of the Palace who had the say,
But Mayors were only bishops. (Grimoald had tried
To rule without them: he soon and violently died.)
So from dawn till dusk they made their triumphal progression,
While war-horns dindled the heavens, silken banners
Flapped in the wind, and the rapt tribes shouted away.

But when darkness fell and their special outing was ended,
Off they were packed again to their secluded manors,
Closely watched day and night to prevent the danger
Of their escaping or talking too much to a stranger,
With nothing to do but affix their seals to charters
They had never been taught to read, and supplied with **plenty**
Of beef and beer and girls from which, as was intended,
They died young, most before they were twenty.

May we not justly call them political martyrs?

Partition

Unbiassed at least he was when he arrived on his mission,
Having never set eyes on this land he was called to partition
Between two peoples fanatically at odds,
With their different diets and incompatible gods.
"Time," they had briefed him in London, "is short. It's too late
For mutual reconciliation or rational debate:
The only solution now lies in separation.
The Viceroy thinks, as you will see from his letter,
That the less you are seen in his company the better,
So we've arranged to provide you with other accommodation.
We can give you four judges, two Moslem and two Hindu,
To consult with, but the final decision must rest with you."

Shut up in a lonely mansion, with police night and day
Patrolling the gardens to keep assassins away,
He got down to work, to the task of settling the fate
Of millions. The maps at his disposal were out of date
And the Census Returns almost certainly incorrect,
But there was no time to check them, no time to inspect

Contested areas. The weather was frightfully hot,
And a bout of dysentery kept him constantly on the trot,
But in seven weeks it was done, the frontiers decided,
A continent for better or worse divided.

The next day he sailed for England, where he quickly forgot
The case, as a good lawyer must. Return he would not,
Afraid, as he told his Club, that he might get shot.

August 1968

The Ogre does what ogres can,
Deeds quite impossible for Man,
But one prize is beyond his reach,
The Ogre cannot master Speech.
About a subjugated plain,
Among its desperate and slain,
The Ogre stalks with hands on hips,
While drivel gushes from his lips.

Fairground

Thumping old tunes give a voice to its whereabouts
long before one can see the dazzling archway
of colored lights, beyond which household proverbs
cease to be valid,

a ground sacred to the god of vertigo
and his cult of disarray: here jeopardy,
panic, shock, are dispensed in measured doses
by foolproof engines.

As passive objects, packed tightly together
on Roller Coaster or Ferris Wheel, mortals
taste in their solid flesh the volitional
joys of a seraph.

Soon the Roundabout ends the clumsy conflict
of Right and Left: the riding mob melts into
one spinning sphere, the perfect shape performing
the perfect motion.

Mopped and mowed at, as their train worms through a tunnel.
by ancestral spooks, caressed by clammy cobwebs,
grinning initiates emerge into daylight
as tribal heroes.

Fun for Youth who knows his libertine spirit
is not a copy of Father's, but has yet to
learn that the tissues which lend it stamina,
like Mum's, are bourgeois.

Those with their wander-years behind them, who are rather
relieved that all routes of escape are spied on,
all hours of amusement counted, requiring
caution, agenda,

keep away:—to be found in coigns where, sitting
in silent synods, they play chess or cribbage,
games that call for patience, foresight, maneuver,
like war, like marriage.

River Profile

Our body is a moulded river

NOVALIS

Out of a bellicose fore-time, thundering
head-on collisions of cloud and rock in an
up-thrust, crevasse-and-avalanche, troll country,
deadly to breathers,

it whelms into our picture below the melt-line,
where tarns lie frore under frowning cirques, goat-bell,
wind-breaker, fishing-rod, miner's-lamp country,
already at ease with

the mien and gestures that become its kindness,
in streams, still anonymous, still jumpable,
flows as it should through any declining country
in probing spirals.

Soon of a size to be named and the cause of
dirty in-fighting among rival agencies,
down a steep stair, penstock-and-turbine country,
it plunges ram-stam,

to foam through a wriggling gorge incised in softer
strata, hemmed between crags that nauntle heaven,
robber-baron, tow-rope, portage-way country,
nightmare of merchants.

Disemboguing from foothills, now in hushed meanders,
now in riffling braids, it vaunts across a senile
plain, well-entered, chateau-and-cider-press country,
its regal progress

gallanted for a while by quibbling poplars,
then by chimneys: led off to cool and launder
retort, steam-hammer, gasometer country,
it changes color.

Polluted, bridged by girders, banked by concrete,
now it bisects a polyglot metropolis,
ticker-tape, taxi, brothel, foot-lights country,
à-la-mode always.

Broadening or burrowing to the moon's phases,
turbid with pulverized wastemantle, on through
flatter, duller, hotter, cotton-gin country
it scours, approaching

the tidal mark where it puts off majesty,
disintegrates, and through swamps of a delta,
punting-pole, fowling-piece, oyster-tongs country,
wearies to its final

act of surrender, effacement, atonement
in a huge amorphous aggregate, no cuddled
attractive child ever dreams of, non-country,
image of death as

a spherical dew-drop of life. Unlovely
monsters, our tales believe, can be translated
too, even as water, the selfless mother
of all especials.

Insignificant Elephants

Although He was the greatest, Our Lord Jesus Christ was made the Most Insignificant of all the Elephants.

THE BESTIARY

Talented creatures, on the defensive because
Glory, Real Estate, Girls, are not in Virtue's gift,
translate into verse or prose,

do equally well in tragic and comic parts,
give storytellers the nudge to invent that cooks
get from slightly-tainted meat.

But a *Hugh of Lincoln* or a *Peter Claver*
are only game for reporters, news, like *Auschwitz,*
Dickens could not have made up

nor *Halley* have predicted: genetic typos
bring forth infant prodigies, imbeciles, midgets,
but no Prime Numbers, no Saints.

Nor would a snapshot reveal a halo: they hide
their incandescence like tasty moths who mimic
unpalatable cousins.

Wild converts, at sea on a collapsing culture,
concocted one or two viable folk tales—*George*
cuts a dash with his Dragon—

but a deal of both semi-gnostic compost-heaps
where spurious cults could mushroom: there never was
a *Catherine* with a Wheel,

nor a *Barbara* to bless the Artillery,
nor an *Uncumber* for English wives to invoke
against lickerous husbands.

Some anecdotes, even from those dark years, have reached us
that are odd enough to be true:—*Perpetua*,
with a beastly end to face,

trying to convince, *Papa, if that is a jug,
I am a Christian,* and dreaming of a shepherd
who consoled her with cream cheese.

With all our flair for research we are still nonplussed:
what shifted members of our species to become
insignificant elephants?

A hard life, often a hard death, and side effects
that a humanist finds hard to stomach, are signs
which divulge nothing. A trait

which might cannot be checked on: all who met them speak
of joy which made their own conveniences
mournfulness and a bad smell.

If their hunch was not mistaken, it would explain
why there is something fishy about a High Style
and the characters it suits,

why we add the embarrassing prefix *super-*
to a natural life which nothing prevents us
living except our natures.

Ode to Terminus

The High Priests of telescopes and cyclotrons
keep making pronouncements about happenings
    on scales too gigantic or dwarfish
    to be noticed by our native senses,

discoveries which, couched in the elegant
euphemisms of algebra, look innocent,
    harmless enough but, when translated
    into the vulgar anthropomorphic

tongue, will give no cause for hilarity
to gardeners or housewives: if galaxies
    bolt like panicking mobs, if mesons
    riot like fish in a feeding-frenzy,

it sounds too like Political History
to boost civil morale, too symbolic of
    the crimes and strikes and demonstrations
    we are supposed to gloat on at breakfast.

How trite, though, our fears beside the miracle
that we're here to shiver, that a Thingummy
        so addicted to lethal violence
        should have somehow secreted a placid

tump with exactly the right ingredients
to start and to cocker life, that heavenly
        freak for whose manage we shall have to
        give account at the Judgment, our Middle-

Earth, where Sun-Father to all appearances
moves by day from orient to occident,
        and his light is felt as a friendly
        presence not a photonic bombardment,

where all visibles do have a definite
outline they stick to, and are undoubtedly
        at rest or in motion, where lovers
        recognize each other by their surface,

where to all species except the talkative
have been allotted the niche and diet that
        become them. This, whatever micro-
        biology may think, is the world we

really live in and that saves our sanity,
who know all too well how the most erudite
        mind behaves in the dark without a
        surround it is called on to interpret,

how, discarding rhythm, punctuation, metaphor,
it sinks into a driveling monologue,
        too literal to see a joke or
        distinguish a penis from a pencil.

Venus and Mars are powers too natural
to temper our outlandish extravagance:
   You alone, Terminus the Mentor,
      can teach us how to alter our gestures.

God of walls, doors and reticence, nemesis
overtakes the sacrilegious technocrat,
   but blessed is the City that thanks you
      for giving us games and grammar and meters.

By whose grace, also, every gathering
of two or three in confident amity
   repeats the pentecostal marvel,
      as each in each finds his right translator.

In this world our colossal immodesty
has plundered and poisoned, it is possible
   You still might save us, who by now have
      learned this: that scientists, to be truthful,

must remind us to take all they say as a
tall story, that abhorred in the Heav'ns are all
   self-proclaimed poets who, to wow an
      audience, utter some resonant lie.

Four Commissioned Texts

RUNNER

(Commentary for a film, directed by Donald Owen and produced by The National Film Board of Canada.)

First Voice   Excellence is a gift: among mankind
To one is assigned a ready wit,
To another swiftness of eye or foot.

Art which raises Nature to perfection
Itself demands the passion of the elect
Who expect to win.

As Pindar long ago in Greece was proud to hail
Thessalian Hippokleas, even so
It is meet we praise in our days fleet-footed
Bruce Kidd from Toronto.

Announcer   The Place of Training: The East York Track Club.
The Trainer: Fred Foote.
The Training Schedule: two hours a day, six days a
week.
Average distance run per week: one hundred miles.

Second Voice   All visible visibly
Moving things
Spin or swing,
One of the two,
Move, as the limbs
Of a runner do,
To and fro,
Forward and back,
Or, as they swiftly
Carry him,
In orbit go
Round an endless track:
So, everywhere, every
Creature disporting
Itself according
To the law of its making,
In the rivals' dance
Of a balanced pair,
Or the ring-dance
Round a common center,
Delights the eye
By its symmetry
As it changes place,
Blessing the unchangeable
Absolute rest
Of the space all share.

First Voice Speed is inborn in sprinter's muscle,
But long learning alone can build
Stamina and strength.
Second Voice   By instruction only
Can limbs learn to live their movements
Without thinking.
First Voice   All important

Is leg-action: arms are for balance.

Second Voice   Of more moment is mileage run
Than time taken.

Announcer   Now for the main event of this Dominion Day
Celebration in East York:
The Two-mile Invitation Race.

We have three international track stars here this
afternoon:
Lt. Max Truex of the United States Navy in the dark
trunks,
Laszlo Tabori, late of Hungary, in the light trunks,
And, of course,
Toronto's own Bruce Kidd.

The runners are lining up for the start mark:
The officials are ready.
They're off!

They're jockeying for position round the first bend.
Tabori's taking a strong lead.
Kidd's right after him.
Now Truex is moving out in front.
Tabori's coming up strong behind him.
Coming down the straightway now, it's
Tabori
Truex
Kidd.

First Voice   Rivals should ride to the race together,
Be firm friends.

Second Voice   Foolish is he
Who, greedy for victory, grits his teeth,

Frowns fiercely before contests,
And no neighbor.

First Voice   It is nice to win,
But sport shall be loved by losers also:
Foul is envy.

Second Voice   False are those
With warm words for the winner after
A poor race.

First Voice   Pleasing to the ear
Are clapping crowds, but the cold stop watch
Tells the truth.

Second Voice   There is time and place
For a fine performance: Fate forbids
Mortals to be at their best always.
God-given is the great day.

Announcer   Truex is spurting ahead,
But Tabori and Kidd are hot on his heels.
One mile to go.
The runners are maintaining a grueling pace.

Now we have the official standing in the two-mile
                                                    event.

KIDD first
TABORI second
TRUEX third.

Second Voice   The camera's eye
Does not lie,
But it cannot show
The life within,
The life of a runner,
Or yours or mine,
That race which is neither

Fast nor slow,
For nothing can ever
Happen twice,
That story which moves
Like music when
Begotten notes
New notes beget,
Making the flowing
Of Time a growing,
Till what it could be
At last it is,
Where Fate is Freedom,
Grace and Surprise.

THE TWELVE

(Anthem for the Feast of any Apostle.
Music by Sir William Walton)

for CUTHBERT SIMPSON

I

Recitative   Without arms or charm of culture,
Unimportant persons
From an unimportant Province,
They did as the Spirit bid,
Went forth into a joyless world
Of swords and rhetoric
To bring it joy.

Chorus When they heard the Word, some demurred, some were
shocked, some mocked. But many were stirred, and the
Word spread. Dead souls were quickened to life; the
sick were healed by the Truth revealed; released into
peace from the gin of old sin, men forgot themselves in
the glory of the story told by the Twelve.

Then the Dark Lord, adored by this world, perceived
the threat of the light to his might. From his throne he
spoke to his own. The loud crowd, the sedate engines
of State, were moved by his will to kill. It was done. One
by one they were caught, tortured and slain.

II

Solo   O Lord, my God,
Though I forsake Thee,
Forsake me not,
But guide me as I walk
Through the Valley of Mistrust,
And let the cry of my disbelieving absence
Come unto Thee,
Thou who declared unto Moses
I SHALL BE THERE.

III

Chorus Children play about the ancestral graves: the dead no
longer walk.
Excellent still in their splendor are the antique statues:
but can do neither good nor evil.
Beautiful still are the starry heavens: but our Fate is not
written there.
Holy still is Speech, but there is no sacred tongue: the
Truth may be told in all.

Twelve as the winds and months are those who taught
us these things:
Envisaging each in an oval glory, let us praise them all
with a merry noise.

MORALITIES

(Text after Aesop. Music by Hans Werner Henze)

I

Speaker   In the First Age the frogs dwelt
At peace in their pond: they paddled about,
Flies they caught and fat grew.

Courts they knew not, nor kings nor servants,
No laws they had, nor police nor jails:
All were equal, happy together.

The days went by in unbroken calm:
Bored they grew, ungrateful for
Their good luck, began to murmur.

Chorus   Higgledy-Piggledy,
What our Society
Needs is more Discipline,
Form and Degree.
Nobody wants to live
Anachronistically:

Lions have a Hierarchy,
Why shouldn't we?

Speaker To mighty Jove on his jeweled throne
Went the Frog-Folk, the foolish people:
Thus they cried in chorus together.

Chorus Hickory-Dockery,
Greatest Olympian,
Graciously grant the pe-
-tition we bring.
Life as we know it is
Unsatisfactory,
We want a Monarchy,
Give us a King!

Bass Solo Foolish children, your choice is unwise.
But so be it: go back and wait.

Speaker Into their pond from the heavens above,
With a splendid splash that sprayed them all,
Something fell, then floated around.

From the edge of their pond in awe they gazed,
The Frog-Folk, the foolish people:
Words they awaited, but no words came.

Chorus He has no legs. He has no head.
Is he dumb? Is he deaf? Is he blind? Is he dead?

It's not a man. It's not a frog.
Why, it's nothing but a rotten old log!
Silly stump, watch me jump!
Tee-hee-hee, you can't catch me!
Boo to you! Boo! Boo! Boo!

Speaker   Back to Jove on his jeweled throne
Went the Frog-Folk, the foolish people:
Thus they cried in chorus together.

Chorus   Jiggery-Pokery,
Jove, you've insulted the
Feelings of every
Sensitive frog:
What we demand is a
Plenipotentiary
Sovereign, not an in-
animate log.

Bass Solo By the hard way must the unwise learn.
So be it: go back and wait.

Speaker   Onto their pond from the heavens above,
Cruel-beaked, a crane alighted.
Fierce, ravenous, a frog-eater.

Doom was upon them, Dread seized
The Frog-Folk, the foolish people:
They tried to escape. It was too late.

Chorus　No! No! Woe! Woe! O! O! O ...

Speaker　If people are too dumb to know when all is well with
them,
The gods shrug their shoulders and say:—To Hell with
them.

II

Speaker　When first had no second, before Time was,
Mistress Kind, the Mother of all things,
Summoned the crows: they crowded before Her.

Alto Solo　Dun must you be, not dainty to behold,
For your gain, though, I grace you with the gift of
song:
Well shall you warble, as welcome to the ear
As the lively lark or loud nightingale.
Go in peace.

Speaker　　　　　　　Gaily they went,
And daily at dawn with dulcet voices
Tooted in the treetops a tuneful madrigal.

Chorus　Now, glorious in the East, the day is breaking:
Creatures of field and forest, from your sleep awaking,
Consort your voices, fearless of exposure,
And of yourselves now make a free disclosure,
Your pitch of presence to the world proclaiming,
Expressing, affirming, uttering and naming,
And each in each full recognition finding,

No scornful echo but a warm responding,
Your several notes not harsh nor interfering,
But all in joy and concord co-inhering.

Speaker So they chanted till by chance one day
Came within earshot where the crows were nesting
A stand of horses, stallions and mares,
Whinnying and neighing as their wont in Spring is.

Chorus How strange! How astonishing! What astonishing
sounds!
Never have we heard such noises as these.
It's so ... so ... so ... so ... so IT!
How new, How new! We must be too. What a break-
through!
Away with dominant and tonic!
Let's be chic and electronic.
Down with the Establishment!
Up with non-music, the Sound-Event!
Arias are out and neighing is in:
Hurrah for horses! Let us begin.

Speaker But crows are no more horses than chutney is tabasco:
Their efforts at *aggiornamento* ended in fiasco.

Chorus CAW! CAW! CAW. CAW! CAW!

III

Speaker A ship put to sea, sailed out of harbor
On a peaceful morning with passengers aboard.

The sun was shining, but the ship's Captain,
Weather-wise, watching the sky,
Warned his crew.

Bass Solo   Wild will be tonight
With a gurling gale and great waves.
To your storm stations! Stand by!

Chorus   O Captain, Captain, tell us the truth!
Are we doomed to drown in the deep sea?

Bass Solo While my body breathes I will battle for our lives,
But our fate lies now in Neptune's hands.

Chorus   Ah: What shall we do? The ship is about to founder,
Overwhelmed by the waves that so wildly surround her.
Neptune at our sins is righteously offended:
Over the deck his dreadful trident is extended.

Neptune, Neptune, forgive us! We confess it sadly,
We have neglected Thy worship and acted very badly.
Forgive us! Have mercy, have mercy, and be our
Saviour,
And for ever after we will alter our behavior.

Neptune, thou Strong One, stop this outrageous welter,
Restrain the wind and waft us safely into shelter:
Bulls we will bring to Thine altar and incense offer,
With treasures of great pride fill up Thy temple coffer.

Bass Solo The wind is falling, the waves are less,
    The clouds scatter, the sky lightens:
    By the kindness of Neptune we have come through.

Chorus We knew He was joking, not serious:
    Who would harm nice people like us?

    In this merry month of May,
      Dew on leaves a-sparkle,
    Of youth and love and laughter sing,
      Dancing in a circle.

    Over hill, over dale,
      Over the wide water,
    Jack McGrew is come to woo
      Jill, the oil-king's daughter.

    Come from afar in his motorcar,
      Eager to show devotion,
    Looking so cute in his Sunday Suit,
      and smelling of shaving lotion.

    Here comes the Bride at her Father's side,
      Fresh as thyme or parsley:
    Blushing now, to the Bridegroom's bow
      She answers with a curtsey.

Boys Semi-Chorus Kiss her once, kiss her twice,
      Bring her orchids on a salver,
      Spit in her eye if she starts to cry,
      And send her to Charlie Colver.

Girls Semi-Chorus Feed the brute eggs and fruit,
Keep him clean and tidy,
Give him what-for if he starts to snore,
And scold him every Friday.

Chorus   We wish you health, we wish you wealth,
And seven smiling children,
Silver-bright be every night,
And every day be golden.

Captain, why do you sit apart,
Frowning over your nautical chart?
Blue is the sky and bright is the sun:
Leave your bridge and join the fun.

Bass Solo   The sky is blue, the sun is bright,
But who laughs in the morning may weep before
night.

Chorus   Your gloom does not enlighten us:
We will not let you frighten us.

An acid-drop for the Corner Cop,
A crab apple for Teacher,
Some moldy fudge for His Honor the Judge,
And a Bronx Cheer for the Preacher.

Speaker   When afraid, men pray to the gods in all sincerity,
But worship only themselves in their days of prosperity.

114

A REMINDER

(Prologue for Christ Church Son et Lumière. Summer 1968)

Mr. Dean, Canons and Students of Christ Church, Ladies and Gentlemen, in lieu of prologue a reminder.

Truth is a single realm, but its governance is a Dual Monarchy.

Tonight we are to take our pleasure in that moiety which lies under the especial care of DAME PHILOLOGY, where persons with Proper Names choose to say and do certain things when, had they so wished, they could have said and done others, where to hear is to translate and to know is to be known.

But, before settling down to enjoy Her lively company, it is meet that we remember to give homage and fair attribution to one who cannot be with us on this occasion, Her co-parcener in wisdom and in this University co-regent, Her younger but no less august and humane sister, DAME ALGEBRA.

Praise Her because, mute but full of sentience, Her written structures exemplify the patterns it is their purpose to convey, and so are read the same by all minds.

Praise Her because She can so elegantly summarize the average effect of anonymous and seemingly disorderly occurrences.

Hers the pure joy of knowing what at all times and in all places is the case: Hers the music, silent and uncarnal, of immortal necessity.

Woe to us if we speak slightingly of Her. Except Her grace prevent, we are doomed to idolatry, to worship imaginary gods of our own childish making, creatures of whim both cruel and absurd.

For She it is, and She alone who, without ambiguity or palter, can teach us to rejoice in the holy Providence of our Creator and our Judge.

Honor to Her, then, and delight to those who serve Her faithfully.
But to Her Sister's revels now. Let music strike!

Prologue at Sixty

for FRIEDRICH HEER

Dark-green upon distant heights
the stationary flocks foresters tend,
blond and fertile the fields below them:
browing a hogback, an oak stands
post-alone, light-demanding.

Easier to hear, harder to see,
limbed lives, locomotive,
automatic and irritable,
social or solitary, seek their foods,
mates and territories while their time lasts.

Radial republics, rooted to spots,
bilateral monarchies, moving frankly,
stoic by sort and self-policing,
enjoy their rites, their realms of data,
live well by the Law of their Flesh.

All but the youngest of the yawning mammals,
Name-Giver, Ghost-Fearer,

maker of wars and wisecracks,
a rum creature, in a crisis always,
the anxious species to which I belong,

whom chance and my own choice have arrived
to bide here yearly from bud-haze
to leaf-blush, dislodged from elsewhere,
by blood barbarian, in bias of view
a Son of the North, outside the *limes*.

Rapacious pirates my people were,
crude and cruel, but not calculating,
never marched in step nor made straight roads,
nor sank like senators to a slave's taste
for grandiose buildings and gladiators.

But the Gospel reached the unroman lands.
I can translate what onion-towers
of five parish churches preach in Baroque:
to make One, there must be Two,
Love is substantial, all Luck is good,

Flesh must fall through fated time
From birth to death, both unwilled,
but Spirit may climb counterwise
from a death, in faith freely chosen,
to resurrection, a re-beginning.

And the Greek Code got to us also:
a Mind of Honor must acknowledge
the happy eachness of all things,
distinguish even from odd numbers,
and bear witness to what-is-the-case.

East, West, on the Autobahn
motorists whoosh, on the Main Line
a far-sighted express will snake by,
through a gap granted by grace of nature:
still today, as in the Stone Age,

our sandy vale is a valued passage.
Alluvial flats, flooded often,
lands of outwash, lie to the North,
to the South litters of limestone alps
embarrass the progress of path-seekers.

Their thoughts upon ski-slope or theatre-opening,
few who pass us pay attention
to our squandered hamlets where at harvest time
chugging tractors, child-driven,
shamble away down sheltered lanes.

Quiet now but acquainted too
with unwelcome visitors, violation,
scare and scream, the scathe of battle:
Turks have been here, Boney's legions,
Germans, Russians, and no joy they brought.

Though the absence of hedgerows is odd to me
(no Whig landlord, the landscape vaunts,
ever empired on Austrian ground),
this unenglish tract after ten years
into my love has looked itself,

added its names to my numinous map
of the *Solihull* gas-works, gazed at in awe
by a bronchial boy, the *Blue John Mine*,

the *Festiniog* railway, the *Rhayader* dams,
Cross Fell, Keld and *Cauldron Snout,*

of sites made sacred by something read there,
a lunch, a good lay, or sheer lightness of heart,
the *Fürbringer* and the *Friedrich Strasse,*
Isafjördur, Epomeo,
Poprad, Basel, Bar-le-Duc,

of more modern holies, *Middagh Street,*
Carnegie Hall and the *Con-Ed* stacks
on *First Avenue.* Who am I now?
An American? No, a New Yorker,
who opens his *Times* at the obit page,

whose dream images date him already,
awake among lasers, electric brains,
do-it-yourself sex manuals,
bugged phones, sophisticated
weapon-systems and sick jokes.

Already a helpless orbited dog
has blinked at our sorry conceited O,
where many are famished, few look good,
and my day turned out torturers
who read *Rilke* in their rest periods.

Now the Cosmocrats are crashed through time-zones
in jumbo jets to a Joint Conference:
nor sleep nor shit have our shepherds had,
and treaties are signed (with secret clauses)
by Heads who are not all there.

Can Sixty make sense to Sixteen-Plus?
What has my camp in common with theirs,

with buttons and beards and Be-Ins?
Much, I hope. In *Acts* it is written
Taste was no problem at Pentecost.

To speak is human because human to listen,
beyond hope, for an Eighth Day,
when the creatured Image shall become the Likeness:
Giver-of-Life, translate for me
till I accomplish my corpse at last.

INDEX OF FIRST LINES

123

ABOUT THE AUTHOR

WYSTAN HUGH AUDEN was born in York, England, in 1907. He has been a resident of the United States since 1939, and an American citizen since 1946. Educated at Gresham's School, Holt, and at Christ Church, Oxford, he became associated with a small group of young writers in London—among them Stephen Spender and Christopher Isherwood—who were to be recognized as the most promising of the new generation in English letters. He collaborated with Isherwood on several plays, including *The Dog Beneath the Skin* and *The Ascent of F-6* (available as *Two Great Plays* in Vintage Books).

Mr. Auden is the author of several volumes of poetry, including *About the House, Homage to Clio, The Double Man, For the Time Being, The Age of Anxiety, Nones, The Shield of Achilles,* and, with Louis MacNeice, *Letters from Iceland* (reissued by Random House in 1969). His *Selected Poetry* appears in The Modern Library. New editions of *The Orators* and *Collected Shorter Poems* were published in 1967. *Collected Longer Poems* was published in 1969. *The Enchafèd Flood,* three critical essays on the romantic spirit, and a volume of essays, *The Dyer's Hand,* are available in Vintage Books. His most recent volume of essays is *Secondary Worlds.*

Mr. Auden has been the recipient of a number of awards, among them the Pulitzer Prize, the National Book Award, the Bollingen Prize in Poetry, the Guinness Poetry Award and, in 1967, the National Medal for Literature given by the National Book Committee.